CURIOUS CREATURES

TWO LIVES

Written by
Joyce Pope

Illustrated by
Stella Stilwell and Helen Ward

STECK-VAUGHN
L I B R A R Y
A Division of Steck-Vaughn Company

Austin, Texas

Editor: Andy Charman
Designer: Mike Jolley
Picture research: Jenny Faithful

Library of Congress Cataloging-in-Publication Data

Pope, Joyce.
Two lives / written by Joyce Pope:
illustrated by Stella Stilwell and Helen Ward.
p. cm. – (Curious creatures)
Includes index.
Summary: Describes, with emphasis on the larval stage and metamorphosis,
how various amphibians, insects, fishes and other marine animals
change as they grow and mature into adults.
ISBN 0-8114-3153-3
1. Metamorphosis – Juvenile literature. 2. Larvae – Juvenile literature.
3. Developmental biology – Juvenile literature.
[1. Metamorphosis.] I. Stilwell, Stella, ill. II. Ward, Helen, 1962–
ill. III. Title. IV. Series.
QL981.P66   1992   91-17460
591.3–dc20   CIP AC

NOTE TO READER
There are some words in this book that are printed in **bold** type.
A brief explanation of these words is given in the glossary on p. 45.

All living things are given a Latin name when first classified by a scientist.
Some of them also have a common name. For example, the common name
of *Sturnus vulgaris* is common starling. In this book we use other Latin words,
such as larva and pupa. We make these words plural by adding an "e," for
example, one larva becomes many larvae (pronounced lar-vee).

Color separations by Positive Colour Ltd., Maldon, Essex, Great Britain
Printed and bound by L.E.G.O., Vicenza, Italy

1 2 3 4 5 6 7 8 9 0 LE 96 95 94 93 92

CONTENTS

GROWING UP

FROG

TADPOLES

DRAGONFLY

DRAGONFLY NYMPH

All living things change throughout their lives. Usually, the changes are small and gradual, as they are in humans. Some creatures, however, particularly **invertebrates** (animals without backbones), may alter more drastically. The young and the adults look different and live differently. The food they eat, the places in which they live, and the things they do are often completely separate. It is as if they have two lives.

The easiest change to see as animals grow older is that they grow bigger. This often happens very quickly. Young animals usually grow fast because they eat a lot.

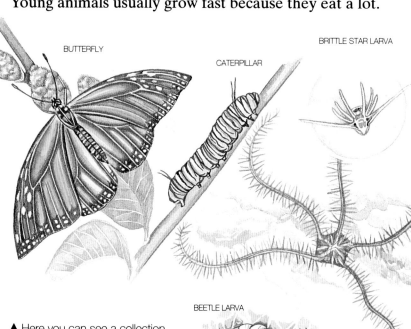

BUTTERFLY

CATERPILLAR

BRITTLE STAR LARVA

BRITTLE STAR

BEETLE LARVA

BEETLE

▲ Here you can see a collection of creatures shown with their **larvae**. (See page 8.) Larvae do not look like their parents. When they change to the shape of the adults, they do so quickly, by **metamorphosis**, as we shall see later.

Big-headed Babies

At birth, a human baby's head takes up about one-third of its total length. Its legs are small and weak. As the baby grows, its head does not get much larger, but its legs become bigger and stronger. A grown-up's head is smaller in proportion and it measures only about one-seventh of the overall height. From this we can see that even humans change a great deal as they grow older.

Sometimes a change in size is all that you can see. A very young earthworm, for instance, is the same shape as an adult, except that it is smaller.

As they grow older, most animals develop reproductive organs. From the time that these organs have developed, the animal is able to produce the next generation of young. Often, other changes take place at the same time. For example, many male birds develop bright feathers when they are fully grown and able to mate. These bright feathers enable the bird to attract a female. Male deer grow antlers when they grow older.

▼ A foal standing beside its mother is nearly as tall as she is because its legs are nearly as long as hers. As it grows older, its legs will get stronger, but not much longer.

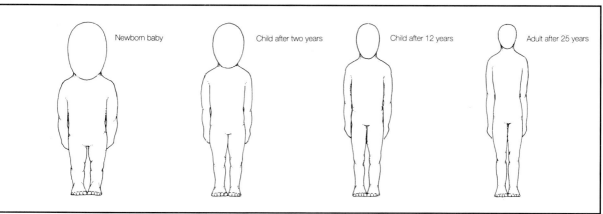

Newborn baby   Child after two years   Child after 12 years   Adult after 25 years

LARVAL LIFE

A **larva** (the plural is larvae) is a young creature that does not look like its parents. Often it is very small compared with the adult. Usually it eats different food and moves about in a different way. When a larva grows up, it changes rapidly to its adult shape.

SEPARATE MEALS

A larva almost always eats different kinds of food from its parents. It may also live in a completely different **habitat** from its parents. This means that although some creatures have large numbers of young, the young do not compete for food or living space with the adults. In some

▶ The larvae of many sea-living creatures form part of the seas' **plankton**. This picture includes some tiny medusae (see pages 40 and 41). The creatures with tufts of hair around their bodies are nauplius larvae of barnacles (see page 42). There are also some small crustaceans, some of which are related to water fleas.

Separate Lives
Adult barnacles cannot move away from their living place but their larvae can. These larvae hatch from eggs and are carried by sea currents to new areas along the coast where they may settle.

Scorpion fly larvae live in a different place from their parents. They are soil-dwellers and feed on small worms. The adults are also hunters but they capture small flying insects, usually in places where there are lots of plants.

The caddis fly larva lives in water. It protects its soft body with a case made of sand grains or bits of vegetation. It feeds mainly on plants. The adult caddis fly eats nothing, though it may drink a little water or take nectar from flowers.

BARNACLE NAUPLIUS LARVA

SCORPION FLY

CADDIS FLY

SCORPION FLY LARVA

CADDIS FLY LARVA

BARNACLES

▼ Swallowtail caterpillars increase in size many times in their few months of life. To do this, they have to eat an enormous quantity of leaves. The adult butterflies do not grow. The food they eat gives them the energy to fly. The sugary **nectar** produced by flowers is an ideal food for this. As it feeds, the butterfly **pollinates** the plant and the plant can make seeds.

cases, the larva is the growing stage of the animal and is little more than a food bag. Sometimes the adults do not eat at all. All of their energy comes from the food they ate when they were larvae. Larvae are often eaten by other animals. Only a small number survive to be adults.

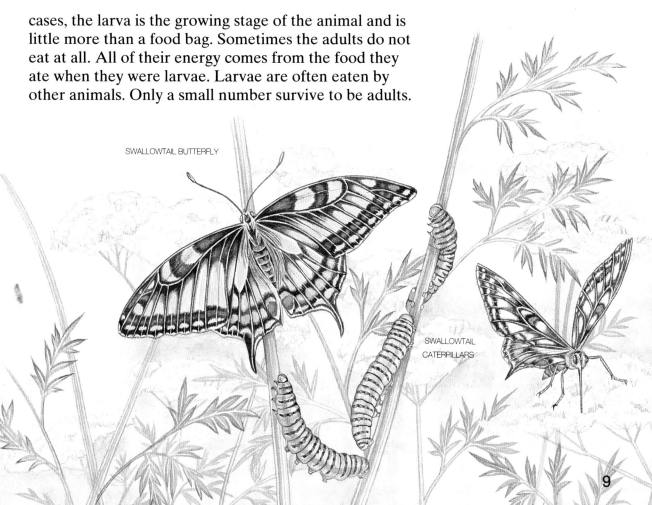

SWALLOWTAIL BUTTERFLY

SWALLOWTAIL CATERPILLARS

FROM LARVA TO ADULT

Many small creatures grow in stages. This is specially so in animals such as insects, spiders, and crabs. These animals do not have an internal skeleton. Instead, they have a hard covering on the outside of their bodies which supports and protects them. They become bigger by **molting**, or shedding, their outer covering. Underneath is a new, soft, covering, which stretches to allow more growth before it too hardens.

Molting is controlled by special chemicals called **hormones**. These are made by **glands**. The glands produce hormones when they are triggered to do so by a change of some kind. Some insects molt if their food supply changes, or when the amount of daylight alters.

The greatest change from larva to adult is called **metamorphosis**. In some kinds of animals this involves losing part of their larval body. The larvae of frogs lose their tails. The **cells** that make up the bodies of insects' larvae are reassembled to make the adult shapes. It is like pulling down a house and using the same bricks to make a very different building.

▲ All insects, such as this cicada, grow by molting. They actually shed their outer skin. The picture above shows an adult emerging from the skin of its young form, which is called a **nymph**.

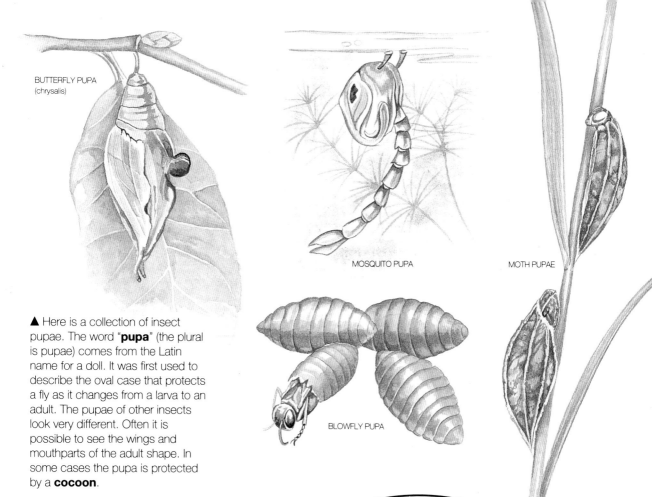

BUTTERFLY PUPA
(chrysalis)

MOSQUITO PUPA

MOTH PUPAE

BLOWFLY PUPA

▲ Here is a collection of insect pupae. The word "**pupa**" (the plural is pupae) comes from the Latin name for a doll. It was first used to describe the oval case that protects a fly as it changes from a larva to an adult. The pupae of other insects look very different. Often it is possible to see the wings and mouthparts of the adult shape. In some cases the pupa is protected by a **cocoon**.

From Egg to Adult

Red admiral butterflies live in much of America, Europe, and Asia. In early summer, females lay their eggs singly on the upper side of stinging nettle leaves. When the caterpillars hatch they spin silk and join the sides of the leaf on which they are feeding. This protects them against many enemies. After feeding for about a month, the caterpillars pupate. Two weeks later, the adult butterfly emerges. Before the butterfly emerges, the pupa splits behind the head as you can see in the photograph to the left. When the insect crawls out, its body is soft and its wings are only 10 percent of their final size. About an hour later they have spread and are hard and dry. Only then can the butterfly fly.

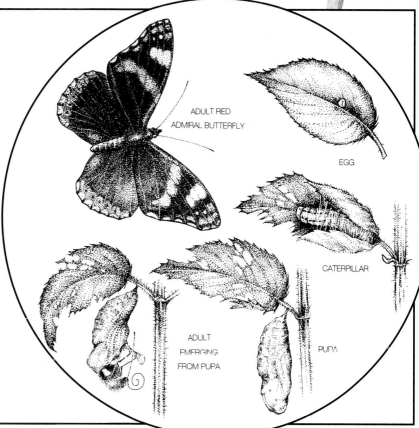

ADULT RED
ADMIRAL BUTTERFLY

EGG

CATERPILLAR

PUPA

ADULT
EMERGING
FROM PUPA

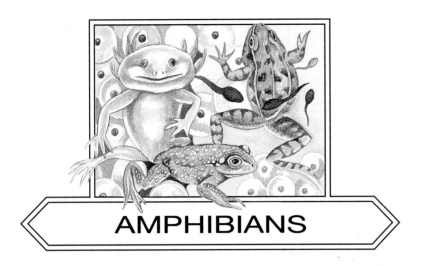

AMPHIBIANS

The name "**amphibian**" means "both ways of life." This refers to the fact that most amphibians spend part of their life in water and part on land. Most amphibians hatch from their eggs into fishlike tadpoles. Like fish, they use **gills** for breathing. Later, they metamorphose, or change, into adults which are capable of living on land. In this way, it can be seen that amphibians actually live two lives.

FROGS AND TOADS

Most frogs are found near water. Adult frogs breathe through small lungs, as well as through their moist skin. Unlike frogs, toads have rough, dry skin. Both frogs and toads are chunky, tailless creatures, with long hind legs, and they hop, rather than walk, on land.

In the breeding season, most frogs and toads find their way to ponds or streams. Here, the females lay large

▶ Common frogs lay clumps of **spawn**, like that shown here, in pools or streams. The water causes the outer covering to swell, making a jellylike protection around the embryos. At first, these look like round black dots but they soon begin to grow. This spawn has been laid about a week. In another week's time the tadpoles will be ready to hatch.

▼ For the first days of its life the tadpole of a common frog does not eat, but hangs on to the jellylike remains of its egg. Once its mouth is open, the tadpole begins to feed on tiny plants and animals. At the same time, it grows feathery gills, though these are soon hidden by a fold of skin. The hind limbs appear when the tadpole is about five weeks old. At the age of about 12 weeks, it loses its gills and tail and becomes a tiny frog.

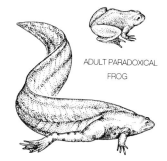

Curious Tadpoles

The tadpoles of paradoxical frogs may be up to 10 inches long. Their parents are only about ¹/₂ inch long.

ADULT PARADOXICAL FROG

TADPOLE OF PARADOXICAL FROG

The tadpoles of swimming-pool frogs have huge gills that lie across the surface of the water.

TADPOLE OF SWIMMING-POOL FROG

numbers of eggs which are **fertilized** by the males after they have been laid. The tadpoles hatch quickly and soon change. First, they lose their gills, then they develop hind legs. Later, front limbs appear. While their limbs grow, their tail shrinks, completing the metamorphosis.

Proteus is a salamander that lives in caves in southern Europe. It is colorless and blind, like many other cave animals. The strangest thing about Proteus is that it keeps a tadpole shape with gills all its life, although it may live for 70 years.

PROTEUS

AMPHIBIAN PARENTS

The egg and tadpole stages of an amphibian's life are full of danger. There are many animals that like to eat them. A few kinds of frogs and toads look after their young at this dangerous time.

In many cases the males help look after the young. Some South American frogs make little swimming pools with mud walls in streams or ponds. Male dart poison frogs carry their tadpoles on their backs, where they get no moisture except from rain. Male nest-making frogs beat the spawn into a meringue-like mass. The outer surface hardens, leaving a moist mass inside. Here the larvae develop and finally wriggle out into a stream. Male marsupial frogs press the fertilized eggs into a pouch on the back of the female. Male Darwin's frogs carry their young in a pouch in their throats until they are able to look after themselves.

Some froglets even complete their tadpole stage inside the egg and hatch as little frogs.

▼ Below you can see some kinds of frogs and toads that look after their tadpoles. Only one of the parents does this. Sometimes it is the mother, but often it is the father. The male midwife toad takes the string of eggs as his mate lays them and drapes them around his body to protect them until they are ready to hatch. Most of the other frogs shown here are also males. But the female marsupial frog carries her babies until they have changed into little frogs and are ready for life on land.

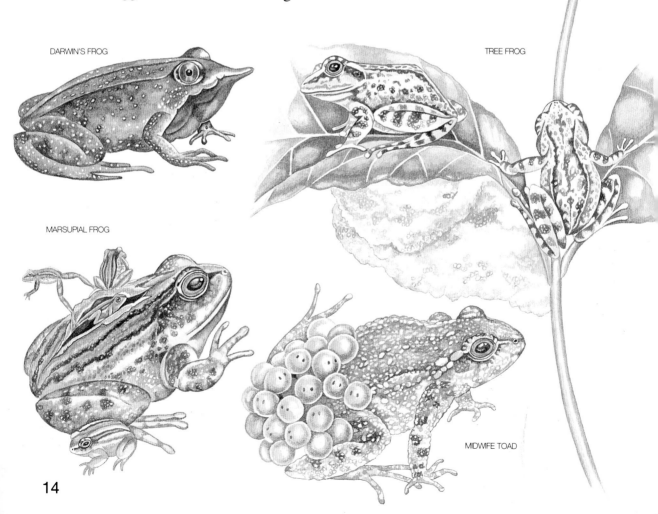

DARWIN'S FROG

TREE FROG

MARSUPIAL FROG

MIDWIFE TOAD

SALAMANDERS

Salamanders look like lizards, but they are amphibians and have a soft, moist skin. Most develop from eggs. These may be laid singly or in clumps and are usually laid in water or hidden in moist places on land. The eggs hatch into active tadpoles that live in water. These tadpoles have gills at first, though these are lost as their lungs develop. The fore, or front, legs of the growing salamanders show first. They do not lose their tails as frogs do. A few kinds of salamander tadpoles never change into the adult shape. They grow large, but look like larvae their whole life.

DUSKY SALAMANDER

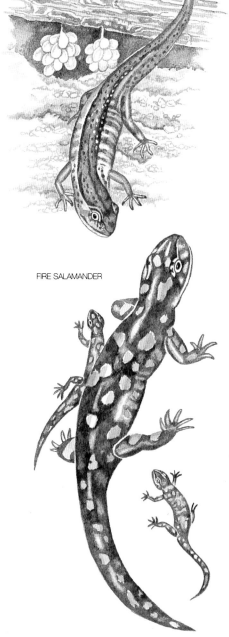

◄ A few kinds of salamanders protect their larvae. Dusky salamanders stay near the place where the eggs are laid and watch over them. Marbled salamanders brood their eggs. Alpine salamanders and some fire salamanders do not lay eggs. The eggs develop and grow into little salamanders before they are born.

▼ This European fire salamander has a small family. Her eggs begin to grow inside her body, and tadpoles with long, ribbonlike gills develop. These are able to take oxygen from their mother's blood. The young are usually born before their gills disappear. However, in a few cases, they metamorphose before birth.

FIRE SALAMANDER

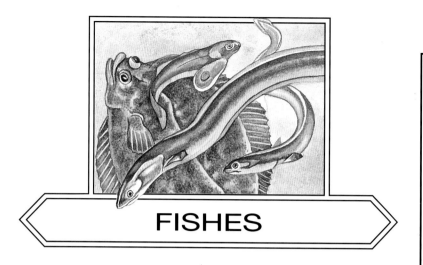

FISHES

Most fishes lay eggs, sometimes in huge numbers. The young that hatch from the tiniest eggs live as larvae for a short time before changing to look like their parents. Young that hatch from bigger eggs take longer to develop into adults. A few fishes, including most sharks, give birth to living young, usually after months of growth inside their mother.

BABY FISHES

Baby fishes usually hatch with a **yolk sac** attached to their bodies. The food in the yolk sac nourishes them as they grow. A newly-hatched salmon, which at first measures a little more than half an inch, remains hidden in the gravel on the bed of a stream for at least a month. In this time, it will grow about a half inch in length and will change shape to look like a little fish.

Larval Fishes

A newly-hatched salmon carries a yolk sac below its body, but it is still recognizable as a fish. Young lampreys are so different from their parents that scientists used to think they were a different species. They bury themselves in sand or mud and feed on tiny creatures. They stay there for three or four years before they change into adults. Many sea fishes, such as the dealfish or the sunfish, grow long spines or tassels during their larval stages. These help to support the young fish in the water.

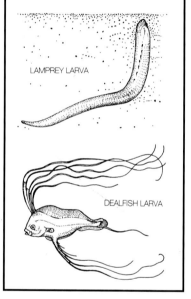

LAMPREY LARVA

DEALFISH LARVA

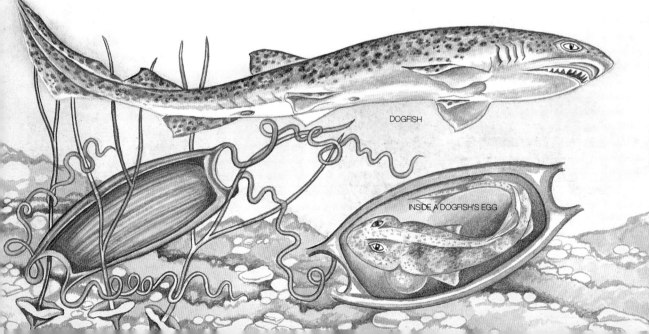

DOGFISH

INSIDE A DOGFISH'S EGG

Some species of fish lay tiny eggs that float in the sea. They hatch into transparent larvae about one-eighth of an inch long. Often, they do not have a mouth or gills and their fins are different from those of the adults. They use up their egg yolk rapidly, and before they are a month old they are shaped like their parents, though they are still only about three-eighths of an inch long.

▶ Salmon feed and grow in the sea, but breed in mountain streams. They frequently travel long distances, against the flow of the water, often through rapids and waterfalls before reaching shallows that are suitable for mating and egg-laying. In some places, their journey is made easier by salmon ladders built by humans to enable the fish to jump up a series of small steps, rather than tire themselves out trying to leap large waterfalls.

▼ Sharks and their relatives, such as the dogfish shown below left, produce either large, living babies or lay big, yolky eggs that take a year to hatch. Butterfishes lay their eggs on the seashore in the winter. The female gathers them together to make a ball about the size of a walnut. She and her mate then take turns guarding them for about a month. When they hatch, the tiny fish drift away as part of the plankton.

BUTTERFISH PROTECTING EGGS

THE AMAZING EEL

Freshwater eels live in ponds and streams in eastern North America and Europe. Other species are found in India, Africa, Australia, and New Zealand. For many centuries eels were mystery fishes, because nobody had ever seen them spawning. All people knew was that each autumn they **migrated** to the sea and in the spring young eels appeared in estuaries and swam upstream. It seemed obvious that they bred in the sea, but nobody knew where.

Long ago, some strange small fishes were discovered. They had flattened, leaflike, transparent bodies and small heads with needlelike teeth. They were called "leptocephalus," a name that means "small head," and people thought that they were just another kind of fish. Then, at the end of the nineteenth century, scientists realized that leptocephaluses were eel larvae.

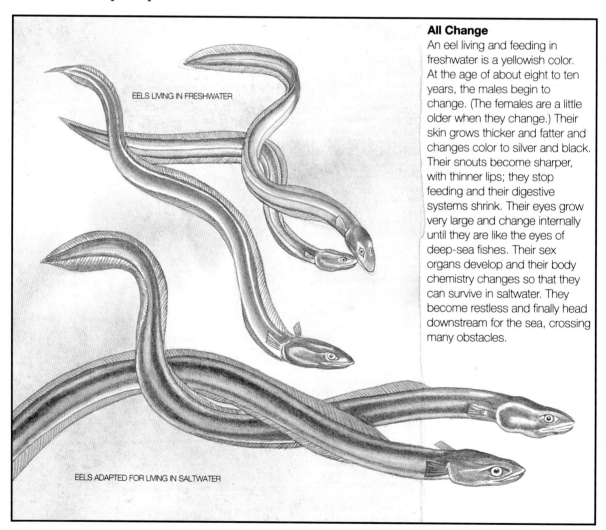

EELS LIVING IN FRESHWATER

EELS ADAPTED FOR LIVING IN SALTWATER

All Change
An eel living and feeding in freshwater is a yellowish color. At the age of about eight to ten years, the males begin to change. (The females are a little older when they change.) Their skin grows thicker and fatter and changes color to silver and black. Their snouts become sharper, with thinner lips; they stop feeding and their digestive systems shrink. Their eyes grow very large and change internally until they are like the eyes of deep-sea fishes. Their sex organs develop and their body chemistry changes so that they can survive in saltwater. They become restless and finally head downstream for the sea, crossing many obstacles.

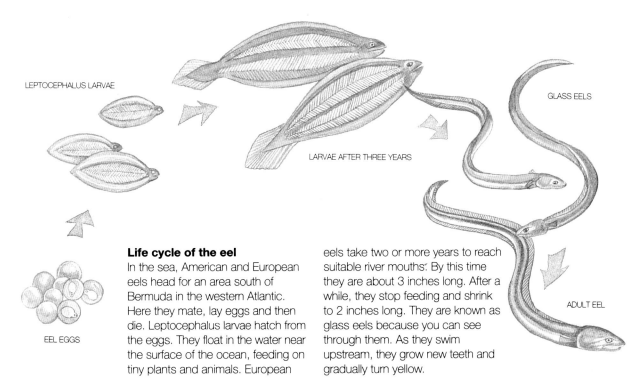

LEPTOCEPHALUS LARVAE

LARVAE AFTER THREE YEARS

GLASS EELS

EEL EGGS

ADULT EEL

Life cycle of the eel

In the sea, American and European eels head for an area south of Bermuda in the western Atlantic. Here they mate, lay eggs and then die. Leptocephalus larvae hatch from the eggs. They float in the water near the surface of the ocean, feeding on tiny plants and animals. European eels take two or more years to reach suitable river mouths. By this time they are about 3 inches long. After a while, they stop feeding and shrink to 2 inches long. They are known as glass eels because you can see through them. As they swim upstream, they grow new teeth and gradually turn yellow.

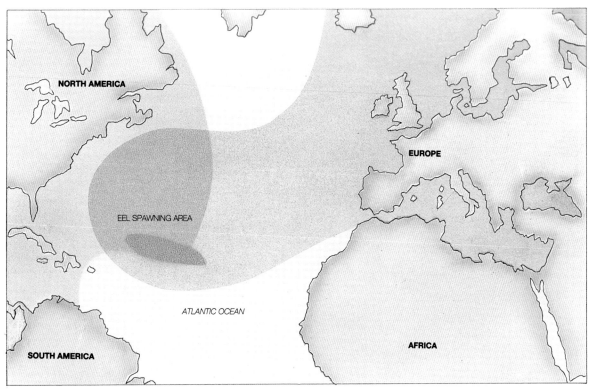

NORTH AMERICA

EUROPE

EEL SPAWNING AREA

ATLANTIC OCEAN

SOUTH AMERICA

AFRICA

▲ American and European eels spend their adult lives in rivers, ponds, and lakes. They travel thousands of miles to the western Atlantic Ocean to spawn. The eggs are laid at depths of about 300 feet. The larvae that hatch from these eggs are carried in ocean currents at depths of between 60 and 160 feet. American eels look similar to European eels but they develop more quickly; they arrive at their destination and metamorphose into their adult form within a year. The European eels travel farther and take over two years to reach the same adult form.

MIGRATION ROUTE OF EUROPEAN EELS

MIGRATION ROUTE OF AMERICAN EELS

MYSTERIOUS LARVAE

Although leptocephalus larvae had been know for over 100 years, scientists did not realize what they were until 1861. Even then, people thought that they were the larvae of ribbonfish rather than eels. Soon after this, they realized their mistake, but they still thought that the larvae were abnormal. Not until the 1890s were scientists convinced that all eels started life in this way.

▲ There are over 600 species of eel. They can be found all over the world, except in the polar region. Most eels live in the sea. They all have long, slender bodies and long dorsal fins. The eel is easy to identify in freshwater. No other fish looks quite like them.

ADULT TARPON

TARPON LARVA

ADULT TEN POUNDER

TEN POUNDER LARVA

Eel Cousins
Adult eels are fairly easy to recognize, because they are all snakelike in shape. Some fishes that look quite unlike adult eels have similar larvae. This may mean that they are related to the eels. Some fish that live in the open sea, such as tarpons and a game fish called the ten pounder, have leptocephalus larvae. Tarpon larvae drift into shallow water in swamps and estuaries. In such places there is not much oxygen and the larvae have to gulp air from the surface. They take to the open sea only when they have changed into the adult form.

FLATFISHES

Adult flatfishes, such as plaice and sole, spend their lives on the ocean bottom. They are beautifully **camouflaged** to match the background of sand or gravel on which they are lying. The females lay large numbers of floating eggs. When these hatch, the tiny fishes that emerge do not look like their parents. They are shaped like "normal" fish, such as herring or goldfish. They swim in the upper waters and feed on tiny animals and plants. After a month or more, one of their eyes starts to move across the head. Both eyes soon lie close together. The mouth grows lopsided, the body flattens and the little fishes begin to swim on one side. Soon they swim down to the ocean floor, where they spend the rest of their lives.

▼ A female plaice lays between 50,000 and half a million eggs, depending on her size. In 10 to 20 days these hatch into larvae one-quarter of an inch long. Hatching and growth take longer if the water is very cold.

PLAICE EGGS

LARVAL PLAICE

A larval plaice grows quickly. It measures one-third of an inch by the time it is three weeks old. Its body is already beginning to flatten and its left eye is moving across the head to lie beside the right eye.

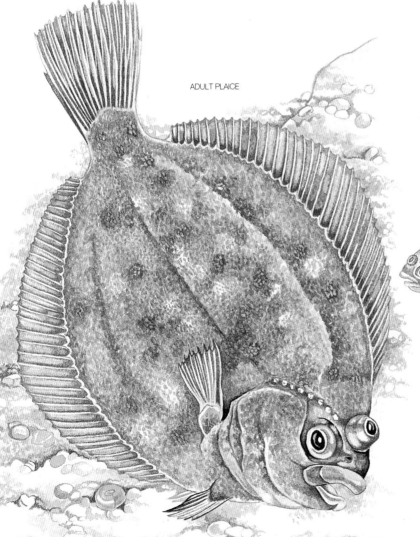

ADULT PLAICE

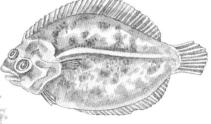

Metamorphosis is complete at the age of one to two months. The little fish measures one-half an inch and lies on its left side in shallow water. Males become adult at about three years old, when they measure about 8 inches long. Females take longer to become adult. They do not spawn until their sixth year, when they are about 14 inches long.

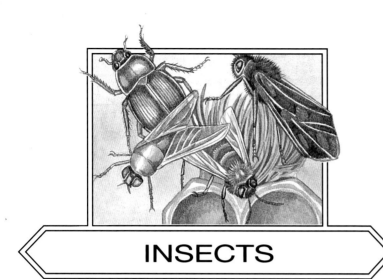

INSECTS

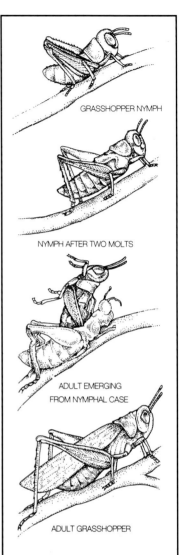

GRASSHOPPER NYMPH

NYMPH AFTER TWO MOLTS

ADULT EMERGING
FROM NYMPHAL CASE

ADULT GRASSHOPPER

Insects and their relatives belong to a huge group of animals called arthropods. Although there are many different kinds of arthropod, they all grow in the same way. This is because they are covered with a hard skin or shell which supports them like a skeleton, and protects them like armor. This cannot stretch as the animal grows. In order to get bigger, arthropods must molt their skin or shell from time to time. This happens very quickly. The armor splits in special places and the creature wriggles out. Every part of the body must be pulled clear, even the eyes and the linings of the breathing tubes. Underneath is a new, soft skin. This stretches as the animal makes itself bigger by swallowing air or water. Then, it hardens to make a strong new armor.

▲ This "ghost insect" is the old skin of a cicada. You can see how the insect pulled itself out of a small slit in the back of its old armor, which even covered its eyes. The hairs are really hollow spines – each one has been pulled clear. The long white strings are the linings of the insect's breathing tubes, which have also been shed.

Growing Wings
Some kinds of insects, including grasshoppers, dragonflies, and earwigs, grow by a process that is called **incomplete metamorphosis**. When this type of insect hatches, it looks like a small version of its parents, but it has no wings. Changes occur as it molts. It gets larger, and bumps appear on its back, showing where the wings are starting to grow. The wings get bigger each time it molts. After a small number of molts the insect is fully grown. It has finished growing and molting. Its wings are free and it can fly and mate.

ADULT DRAGONFLY EMERGING FROM
NYMPHAL CASE

ADULT DRAGONFLY WITH
WINGS EXPANDING

ADULT DRAGONFLY

DRAGONFLIES

The young of insects that grow by incomplete metamorphosis are called nymphs. They usually eat food similar to the adults. Dragonfly nymphs and adults are hunters. The nymph lives in water and catches its **prey** with a special grabbing organ called the mask. This is normally folded under the head, but it can be shot out to capture small fish or other water creatures. The nymph molts several times as it grows and leaves the water for its last molt. Soon after struggling out of the nymphal case, the huge, glistening wings of the adult expand and the creature is ready to start on the last phase of its life. In this final phase, it finds a mate and the female lays eggs.

▼ This newly molted dragonfly nymph still has its old skin beside it. Many kinds of nymphs grow slowly, and in cooler parts of the world they may take up to five years to complete their underwater life. The adult dragonflies survive for only a few months.

BUTTERFLIES AND MOTHS

The eggs laid by butterflies and moths hatch into creatures quite unlike their parents. They are caterpillars, different in color and shape from the adults, unable to fly and needing different food. This is because moths and butterflies are insects that develop by a process called **complete metamorphosis**. They change completely between the growing and the adult stages. The caterpillar, or grub, spends all its time and energy feeding and growing. The job of the adult is to mate and lay eggs.

The caterpillar's vision and other senses are poor, and it can only move slowly. Many caterpillars are wonderfully camouflaged. Others are covered with prickly hairs or taste so horrible that no other animals eat them. Often, they are brightly colored to warn **predators** to leave them alone.

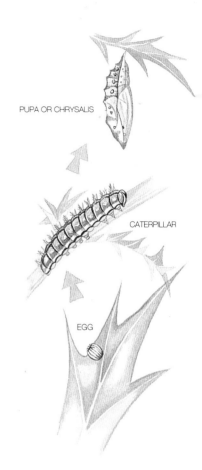

PUPA OR CHRYSALIS

CATERPILLAR

EGG

▼ Silk moths make cocoons that have a papery inner layer, a middle layer formed from a strong thread, and a fluffy outer layer. When the adult moth is ready to emerge, it produces a chemical that dissolves the cocoon. The moth then escapes. In some parts of the world, people unwind the middle layer, which gives them a silk thread about 1,500 feet long.

ADULT BUTTERFLY EMERGING

ADULT BUTTERFLY

▲ Painted lady butterflies lay their eggs in early summer, usually on thistle leaves. They hatch in about a week. The caterpillars are fully grown after about a month and usually hide their pupae, known as **chrysalises**, in the shelter of the spiny leaves of their food plant. The thistle protects them from hungry animals. They spend about two weeks as pupae and then emerge as adults.

▶ Caterpillars of butterflies and moths produce silk from glands in their heads. This silk moth is tying leaves together with a silk thread to make a cocoon in which it can pupate.

Staying Alive

Caterpillars are the favorite food of many small flesh-eaters, including birds, shrews, toads, and lizards. Caterpillars cannot run away from danger, so they defend themselves in other ways. Some feed at night and rest, without moving, by day. They look so much like twigs or other parts of plants that their enemies do not notice them. Others have thick coats of spiny hairs, which make them uneatable. Others have chemicals in their bodies that make them taste bad. Usually these caterpillars are brightly colored, and this acts as a warning to the creatures that might eat them.

SILK MOTH MAKING A COCOON

BEETLES

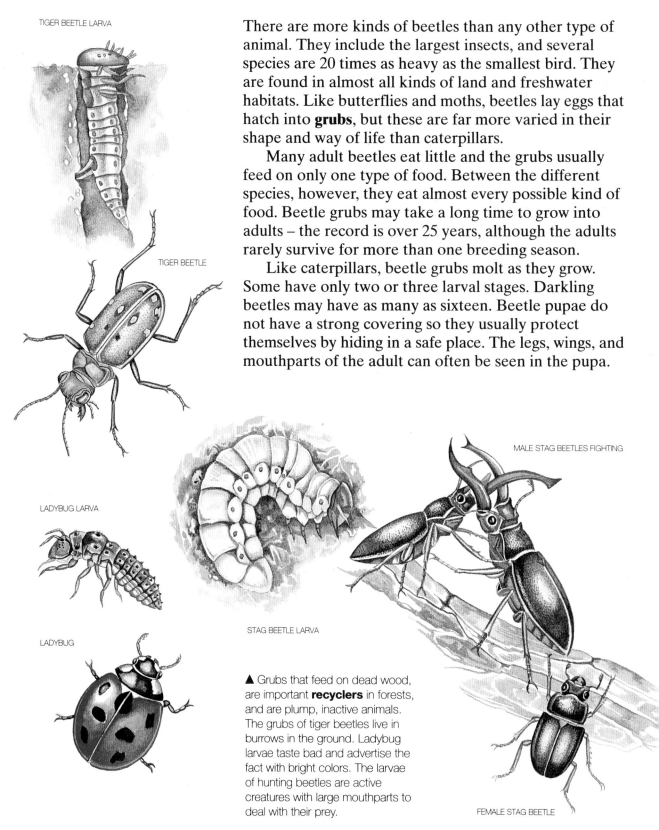

TIGER BEETLE LARVA

TIGER BEETLE

There are more kinds of beetles than any other type of animal. They include the largest insects, and several species are 20 times as heavy as the smallest bird. They are found in almost all kinds of land and freshwater habitats. Like butterflies and moths, beetles lay eggs that hatch into **grubs**, but these are far more varied in their shape and way of life than caterpillars.

Many adult beetles eat little and the grubs usually feed on only one type of food. Between the different species, however, they eat almost every possible kind of food. Beetle grubs may take a long time to grow into adults – the record is over 25 years, although the adults rarely survive for more than one breeding season.

Like caterpillars, beetle grubs molt as they grow. Some have only two or three larval stages. Darkling beetles may have as many as sixteen. Beetle pupae do not have a strong covering so they usually protect themselves by hiding in a safe place. The legs, wings, and mouthparts of the adult can often be seen in the pupa.

MALE STAG BEETLES FIGHTING

LADYBUG LARVA

STAG BEETLE LARVA

LADYBUG

▲ Grubs that feed on dead wood, are important **recyclers** in forests, and are plump, inactive animals. The grubs of tiger beetles live in burrows in the ground. Ladybug larvae taste bad and advertise the fact with bright colors. The larvae of hunting beetles are active creatures with large mouthparts to deal with their prey.

FEMALE STAG BEETLE

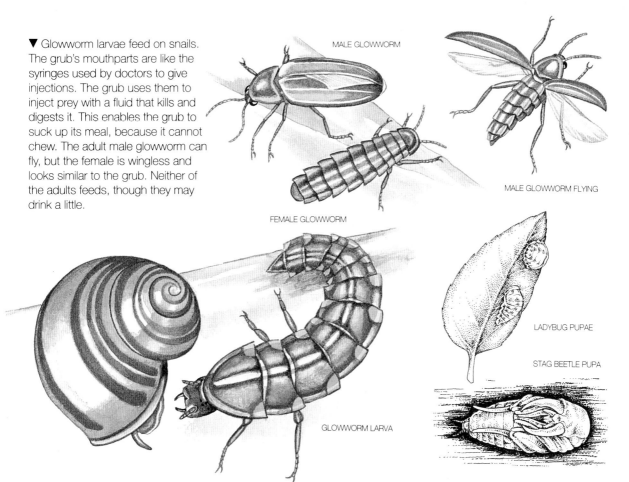

▼ Glowworm larvae feed on snails. The grub's mouthparts are like the syringes used by doctors to give injections. The grub uses them to inject prey with a fluid that kills and digests it. This enables the grub to suck up its meal, because it cannot chew. The adult male glowworm can fly, but the female is wingless and looks similar to the grub. Neither of the adults feeds, though they may drink a little.

MALE GLOWWORM

MALE GLOWWORM FLYING

FEMALE GLOWWORM

LADYBUG PUPAE

STAG BEETLE PUPA

GLOWWORM LARVA

Hitching a Ride

A few beetle larvae are **parasites**. The European blister beetle larvae is one. The beetle's tiny, active larvae, called triungulins, wait in flowers. When a bee visits the flower, the larvae hang onto the bee and are carried back to her nest. A larva must eat one of the bee's eggs to stay alive. It then changes into a blind, maggotlike creature and feeds on the bee's store of honey. Eventually it leaves the nest to pupate in the soil. Its chances of survival are small, because very few kinds of bee are suitable **hosts**. For this reason, blister beetles lay up to 40,000 eggs at one time.

▲ Beetle pupae are not usually able to defend themselves. They have to find some way of being safe from predators. Many, such as the stag beetle shown here, make a special pupation chamber either underground or in the wood on which they have been feeding. This chamber is usually near the surface of the soil or wood because the adult must be able to escape easily when its metamorphosis is complete. Ladybug pupae do not have to hide away because they are able to wriggle violently if something disturbs them.

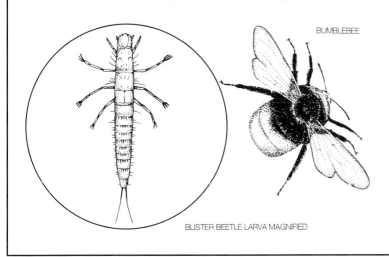

BUMBLEBEE

BLISTER BEETLE LARVA MAGNIFIED

FLIES AND FLEAS

Unlike butterflies and many other insects that have the word "fly" tacked on to their name, true flies have only one pair of wings. Butterflies and dragonflies have two large pairs of wings. In flies, the hind pair of wings has become very tiny and acts as balancers. This is one of the reasons that they can fly so acrobatically.

True flies must be among the most hated of all creatures. Some flies certainly do destroy food stores and others spread disease. These are a minority, however. Flies form one of the largest insect groups and most of them do not affect human beings. Many are useful because they pollinate plants and help to break down the bodies of dead animals.

Although there are a variety of fly larvae, most are maggots. These legless, wriggling creatures are thinner at the front end, which is where the mouthparts are.

Fly pupae are usually enclosed in a tough case. When the adult develops, it escapes by using a blood-filled bladder that develops on its head. It uses this as a battering ram to break its way into the outside world.

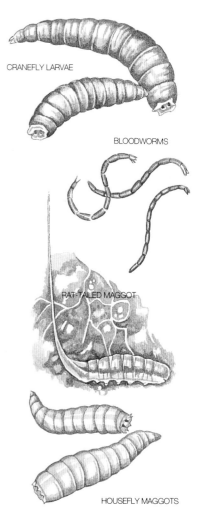

CRANEFLY LARVAE

BLOODWORMS

RAT-TAILED MAGGOT

HOUSEFLY MAGGOTS

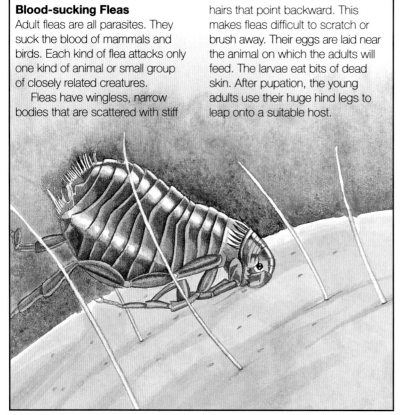

Blood-sucking Fleas

Adult fleas are all parasites. They suck the blood of mammals and birds. Each kind of flea attacks only one kind of animal or small group of closely related creatures.

Fleas have wingless, narrow bodies that are scattered with stiff hairs that point backward. This makes fleas difficult to scratch or brush away. Their eggs are laid near the animal on which the adults will feed. The larvae eat bits of dead skin. After pupation, the young adults use their huge hind legs to leap onto a suitable host.

▲ Leatherjackets, which are the larvae of craneflies, live in the soil. They use biting mouthparts to feed on the roots of grasses and other plants. Some fly larvae develop in water. Bloodworms can survive in places where there is very little oxygen. They feed on decaying vegetation. Mosquito larvae are active swimmers, breathing air through short tubes that they push through the surface of the water. They have brushes of hairs that sweep tiny scraps of food through the water into their mouths. Rat-tailed maggots can live in airless water and breathe through a very long tube. The maggots of short-bodied flies, such as houseflies, mostly live and feed on decaying matter.

Feeding Time for Flies

Flies' mouthparts are in the form of a proboscis, or tube. They are not able to chew. In houseflies, the proboscis is short and ends in a kind of pad. This is used as a filter, through which only liquids or very fine particles of food can pass. The bee fly has a very long proboscis, and the insect can reach nectar that is hidden deep in flowers.

Some flies are hunters. Their proboscis is much stronger and it can pierce the body of their prey. Some flies feed on blood. Often, only the female fly takes blood, because she needs a high protein meal before her eggs are ready to be laid. The males usually feed on plant juices.

Diseases may be spread by bloodsucking insects. Before taking a meal, they pump a chemical into their prey that prevents the blood from clotting. Sometimes these insects are infected with organisms that cause diseases, such as malaria or yellow fever. As it feeds, the infected insect passes those organisms and diseases to its host.

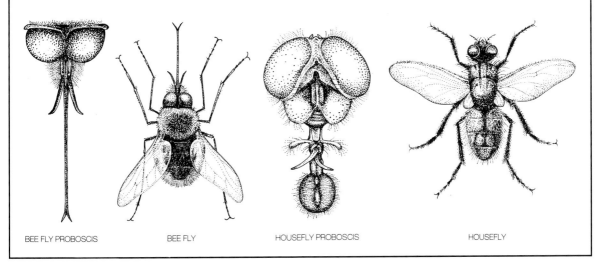

BEE FLY PROBOSCIS   BEE FLY   HOUSEFLY PROBOSCIS   HOUSEFLY

◄ Mosquito larvae hatch from eggs laid in still water. Most of the time they hang from a film on the surface of the water, held there by hairs at the end of their breathing tubes. They do not have limbs or fins, so they swim by frantic wriggling of their bodies. A larva has bunches of fine hairs near its head. By moving these to and fro, it creates small currents in the water. These bring it the tiny plants and animals on which it feeds. Mosquito larvae are important food for fishes and most of them get eaten. Any that survive live for about three weeks and then pupate.

PARENTAL CARE

Most insects do not live long enough to care for their young. The best that they can do is to lay eggs where the larvae will find plenty of food. In some cases, the adults go to a lot of trouble to provide food for their young. Some weevils cut around the bark of the twig where they intend to lay eggs so that the larvae will have the withered leaves they need to feed on. Some adults make a nest for their young. Male and female dung beetles work together to dig a brood chamber. Solitary bees and wasps also care for their young. The female makes the nest and brings food. In a few species she lives long enough to continue providing food until the larvae are fully grown.

▼ Sexton beetles find the remains of freshly dead creatures such as mice and small birds. A male and female work together and dig away at the soil under the corpse, until eventually it is buried. The male may leave after mating, but the female lays a small number of eggs and remains with them. After about five days they hatch, and the female feeds the grubs partly digested food from the corpse. She continues to do so until the grubs have gone through at least two molts. They grow very fast. Their weight doubles in the first seven hours and will have increased 100 times by the time they pupate, seven days later.

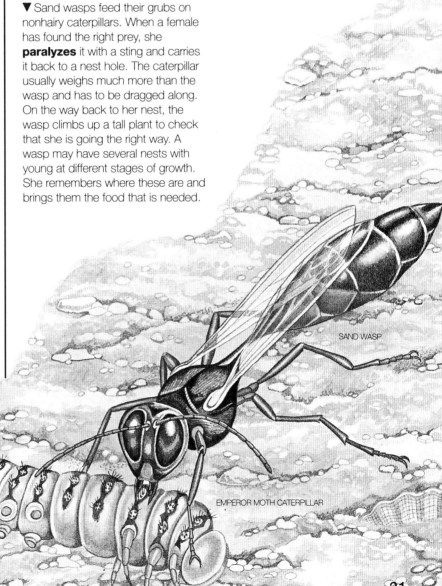

BEES AND WASPS

Solitary bees have shorter lives than honeybees. They care for their grubs by making a nest, and by providing their grubs with **pollen** and honey. In many cases the nest is underground. Often a large number of bees use the same area, but they all work as individuals. Solitary bees are not able to make wax, so the combs, which are small, are formed from leaves or other plant material.

Solitary wasps also provide food for their young. Their nests may be in sandy soil, or in beautiful little clay pots made by the wasps. The young are fed on insects or spiders. Each kind of wasp is a specialist hunter taking only one type of prey.

▼ Sand wasps feed their grubs on nonhairy caterpillars. When a female has found the right prey, she **paralyzes** it with a sting and carries it back to a nest hole. The caterpillar usually weighs much more than the wasp and has to be dragged along. On the way back to her nest, the wasp climbs up a tall plant to check that she is going the right way. A wasp may have several nests with young at different stages of growth. She remembers where these are and brings them the food that is needed.

FEMALE EARWIG WITH EGGS

Earwig Eggs

During the early part of the winter, female earwigs make nests in sheltered places, under stones or in the surface of the soil. Here they lay a small number of eggs. If the mother dies the eggs do not survive because they are quickly attacked by molds which destroy them. The females stay with the eggs, fondling and licking them. This probably keeps them clean and healthy. In the spring, when the young hatch, the females stay with them and feed them for a short time.

SAND WASP

EMPEROR MOTH CATERPILLAR

▼ When a worker honeybee emerges from her pupa in the summer, her first job is to learn her way about the hive. She becomes a housebee, cleaning out cells so that the queen can lay more eggs in them.

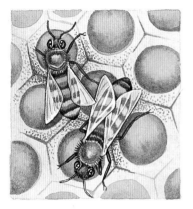

After about three days she becomes a nursemaid, feeding the older larvae on pollen and honey. By her sixth day some glands in her throat have developed and produce a food called "royal jelly." She feeds this to the young larvae.

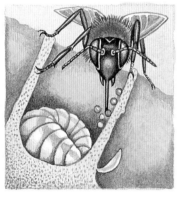

This phase lasts until she is 12 days old. She is able to produce wax at this age. She then becomes a builder, repairing and adding to the honeycomb.

HAPPY FAMILIES

An ants' nest or a hive of bees containing many thousands of insects is simply a huge family. All the insects have the same mother, who is the queen. Insects that live in this way are called social insects. Bumblebees and wasps have a simple social life. A female that has mated survives the winter and starts to make a nest in the spring. She lays eggs and cares for the first grubs. They become workers, which are smaller than their mother. When they are adults they take over the job of running the nest and rearing more young. Later, females and males that can mate are produced. After the birth of these, the nest gradually runs down. The queen dies and so do all the others except the females that have mated. These will start next year's nests.

Other insects that live in colonies include ants, termites, and wasps. Termites commonly tunnel through, and damage, wooden structures, such as houses, fences, and even living trees. In very warm parts of the world, termites live in huge colonies, building mound-shaped nests 20 feet high.

Soon, the bee makes her first trip outside the hive, in a "play flight." This play flight helps her to learn the landmarks around the hive. Inside the hive, she is busy storing pollen and making honey. When she is about 3 weeks old, she starts to collect nectar, pollen, and water. She continues with these jobs until she dies of old age about 3 weeks later.

HONEYBEE COLLECTING
NECTAR AND POLLEN

▲ Wasps' nests are made of paper. This is formed from chewed-up wood. There are a number of horizontal layers, like floors of an apartment building. The combs open downward, so the larvae live an upside-down life. The workers bring them food, usually insects. The grubs give the adults a sugary substance. This picture shows an early stage in the building of a wasp's nest. By the end of the summer it will be bigger than your head.

Colonial Life

Termites are sometimes called "white ants." All termites are social insects, but their lives are quite different from the lives of ants. Termites do not go through a grub stage. The workers are mainly the young. They will grow to be fully sexed adults, or soldiers who protect the colony.

The size of colonies varies, but some species may include several million insects in a single nest. Termites are the only social insects in which the male survives. Like the queen, he probably lives a long time. The queen's body is often hugely swollen with eggs. The male looks tiny beside her.

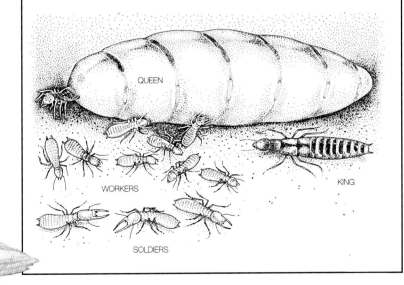

QUEEN

WORKERS

KING

SOLDIERS

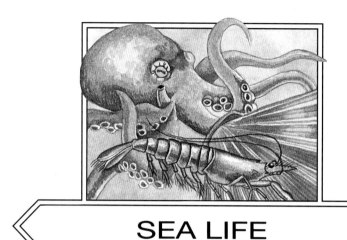

SEA LIFE

Seawater looks clear, but, in fact, it contains millions of tiny plants and animals. Many of the animals are larvae. Most are too small to be seen without a microscope. They are eaten by much larger animals such as the huge basking sharks that reach lengths of up to 40 feet.

THE PLANKTON

Plankton is the name given to the floating life of the sea. Some of the creatures carried by the great ocean currents are large but fragile adults, such as jellyfish. Most, however, are the larvae of freely-moving animals. Often the larvae float away from the area in which their parents

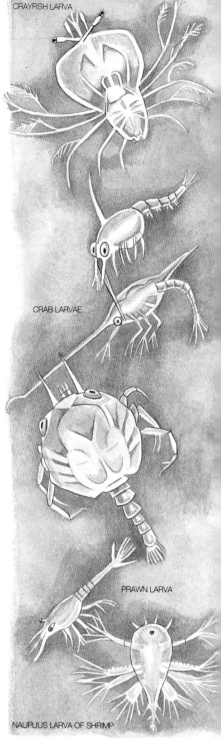

CRAYFISH LARVA

CRAB LARVAE

PRAWN LARVA

NAUPLIUS LARVA OF SHRIMP

Prawn Eyes

Larval prawns swim upside down at the surface of the ocean where there is plenty of light. Prawn larvae have eyes that are made up of many parts and arranged in a honeycomb pattern. They can see very well. When danger, in the form of a fish or other hunter appears, they jerk out of the way. The larva develops into an adult that lives on the ocean floor. Its eyes change as it grows. The honeycomb shapes become square, and are arranged so that light entering the many different parts of the eye is concentrated on a single spot. This means that, although prawns do not have very clear vision, they can see in places where there is not much light.

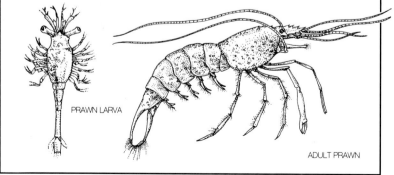

PRAWN LARVA

ADULT PRAWN

▲ Almost any haul of plankton from the ocean will bring in larvae that belong to the lobsters and crabs and their relatives. The long spines on their bodies act like water skis to hold them up in the water. They feed by beating their legs to draw even smaller creatures to their mouths.

live. With luck they may find a place where they will not have to compete with their parents for food or shelter.

Many of the planktonic young change their appearance several times as they prepare for adulthood. Each change enables the tiny larvae to live a slightly different way of life. Unlike the larvae of insects, which are the insects' only growing phase, planktonic animals continue to grow even after they have changed to the adult shape.

Planktonic larvae are some of the strangest-looking of all creatures. Most are transparent, though some glisten with oily rainbows. Some have very flat bodies, and others have long spines that help to keep them from sinking to the ocean floor. Many have minute hairs, called cilia, which they beat like tiny oars, to hold their position in the water. This movement also creates currents that waft food to their mouthparts.

▼ The photograph below shows the larva of a common starfish. It looks quite unlike the adult starfish. This larva forms part of the plankton which is food for many other creatures that live in the sea.

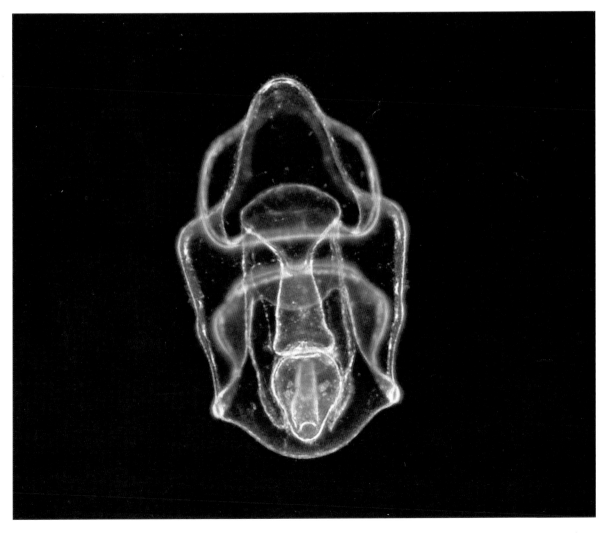

SEASHELL LARVAE

Who could guess that the heavily-armored seashells of the shore start their lives as tiny and unprotected larvae? These larvae float in the open ocean and are in constant danger of being eaten by the many larger animals that surround them.

The first larval stage of a limpet or conch is a simple speck of life. It has a tuft of long hairs, or **cilia**, on the top of its egg-shaped body and a band of cilia running around the middle. As it grows, a tiny shell develops to protect its lower parts.

Sea snails have a ring of cilia that is drawn out to form two great arms above the little shell. These arms give the snail stability and prevent it from spinning around and around. After various changes, the little creature takes on the adult shape and sinks to the ocean bottom. It may continue to grow for many years.

▶ The flame scallop, unlike most bivalves does not bury itself in sand, but lives on the ocean floor. It is even able to swim if it senses danger. In spite of these differences from most other bivalves, the larvae that hatch from the scallop's eggs are like those of other bivalves.

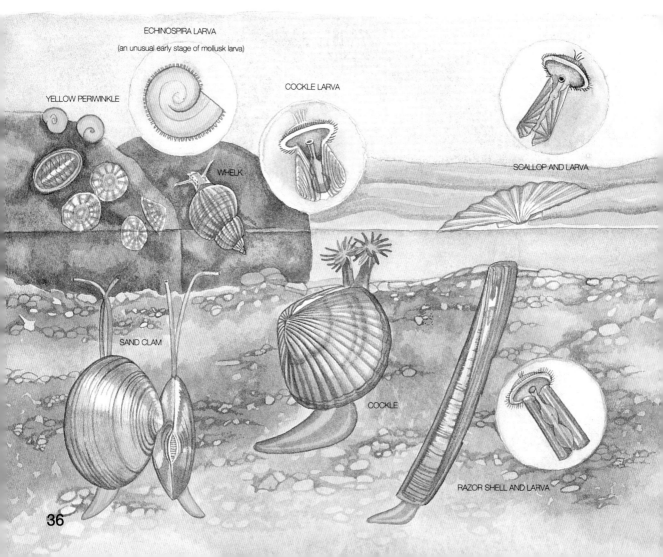

ECHINOSPIRA LARVA
(an unusual early stage of mollusk larva)

YELLOW PERIWINKLE

COCKLE LARVA

WHELK

SCALLOP AND LARVA

SAND CLAM

COCKLE

RAZOR SHELL AND LARVA

Waves of Motion

A cilium (plural: cilia) is a short thread of tissue that sticks out from the cells of many kinds of animals. Cilia usually beat in the liquid that surrounds them. Some creatures, such as the single-celled paramecium shown below, are covered with a short fur of cilia. Others, such as limpet larvae, have cilia in bands around their bodies. Cilia have two main functions. In some creatures they are used to move the animal through a liquid. In others, they move the liquid around the animal, usually to flow food and oxygen toward the mouth.

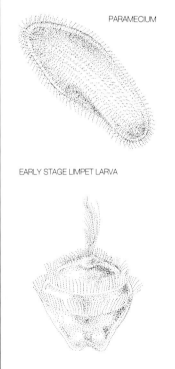

PARAMECIUM

EARLY STAGE LIMPET LARVA

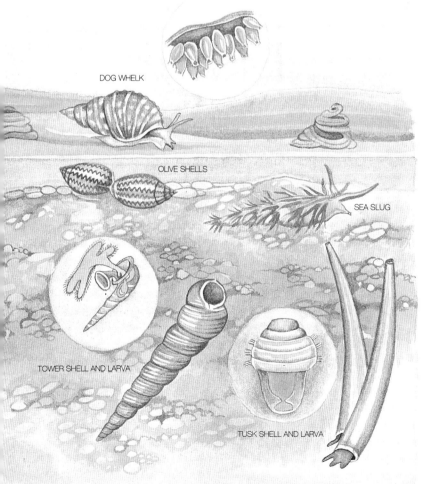

DOG WHELK EGGS

DOG WHELK

OLIVE SHELLS

SEA SLUG

TOWER SHELL AND LARVA

TUSK SHELL AND LARVA

◀ A few of the snails and bivalves that live on the seashore get through their larval life in the shelter of an egg and then hatch as small versions of their parents. Others, like those shown here, have complicated larval lives. Although the larvae are barely visible without a microscope you do not notice them in the water because they are transparent.

STARFISH RELATIVES

Starfishes are related to brittle stars, sea urchins, and sea cucumbers. They are different from most other animals because they are structured on a circular body plan like the spokes of a wheel. Creatures shaped like this are called radially symmetrical animals. They have no head and no tail end, so there is no concentration of brain and sense organs into one main area. They are usually slow moving and sluggish.

Amazingly, the eggs laid by starfishes hatch into tiny creatures that have a left and a right side. At first, they are compact little animals, but as they grow they develop spines that help to support them in the sea. Long bands of cilia looped around their bodies enable them to feed and move. As they grow, part of the left side of the larva develops into the adult shape. This grows its own mouth and nervous system quite apart from that which exists on the other side. Most of the tissues of the larva's body form the new animal; the few remaining parts are cast aside. Finally, the tiny, radially symmetrical starfish sinks to the ocean bottom.

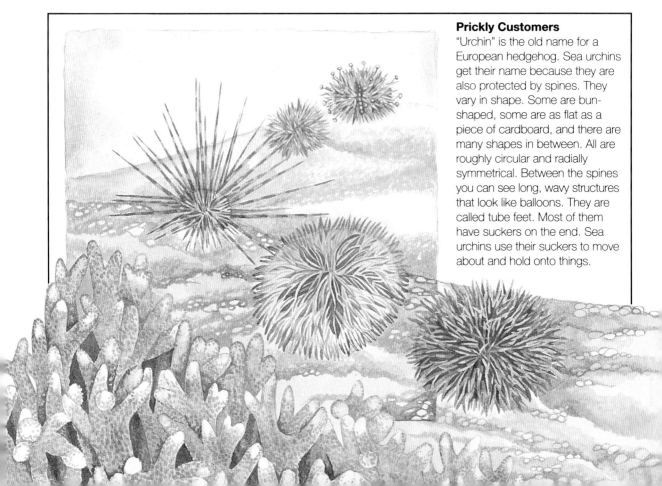

Prickly Customers

"Urchin" is the old name for a European hedgehog. Sea urchins get their name because they are also protected by spines. They vary in shape. Some are bun-shaped, some are as flat as a piece of cardboard, and there are many shapes in between. All are roughly circular and radially symmetrical. Between the spines you can see long, wavy structures that look like balloons. They are called tube feet. Most of them have suckers on the end. Sea urchins use their suckers to move about and hold onto things.

▼ When it first hatches, a starfish larva is almost egg-shaped. A wavy band of cilia runs around its body and helps to stabilize it. It cannot yet feed.

In time, the larva's mouth opens and it can feed. As it grows, the bands of cilia become longer until they become the spines that help support it in the water.

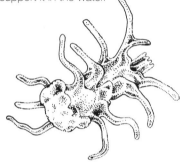

As the adult starfish develops, the larva itself grows smaller. Eventually there is nothing much left except some long, supporting spines. Finally, when it is about as large as a grain of sand, the starfish begins its adult life. The spines drop off and sink to the ocean floor.

▲ The arms of this feather star, like those of its relatives the starfishes, surround its mouth. However, when it changed from its larval stage, it settled on the ocean bottom with its mouth uppermost, not on the underside. Feather stars feed on very small plants and animals that are caught and transported to the mouth down a groove in the center of each arm.

ADULT COMMON STARFISH

TUBE FEET

Adult starfishes usually have five arms, with the body and mouth in the center of them. The tube feet are on the underside of the arms. Sometimes an arm gets broken. The starfish is able to grow another one, which is why you sometimes find starfishes with arms of different lengths.

JELLYFISH

Jellyfish and their relatives are very simple animals. Their bodies are shaped like a bag with tentacles around the opening. In some, the bag opens downward and the animal is known as a medusa. In others, such as sea anemones, the bag opens upward. In this case the creature, which is always fixed to the ocean floor, is called a polyp. Many polyps look like flowers, but they and the medusae are all flesh-eating animals.

These animals produce their young in complex ways. Some are able to bud off babies. Others produce tiny medusalike larvae that float in the water for a short time before changing to their adult form.

► Other jellylike animals include the comb jellies. At night they glow with rainbow colors, and are some of the most beautiful and fragile creatures of the oceans. They spend their whole life as part of the plankton, for most do not produce larvae. Salps are also jellylike animals. They float in the surface of the sea for all of their life, but they are very different from the jellyfish or comb jellies. The larvae that they produce are like tiny tadpoles. Their structure shows that the salps are more closely related to animals with backbones, such as fish and amphibians, than to the jellyfish.

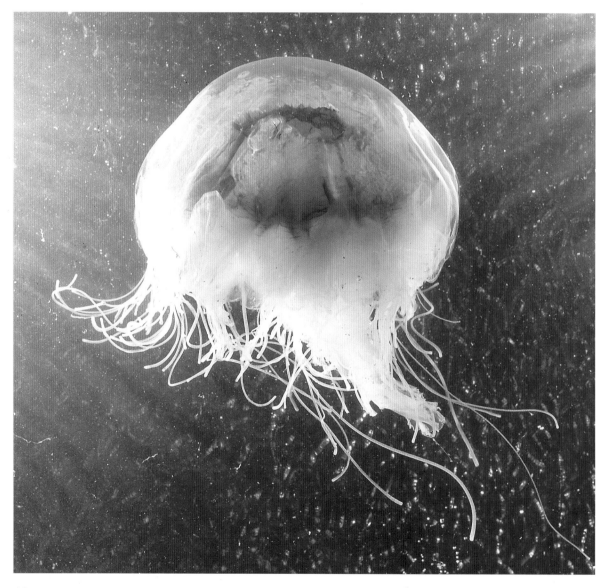

COMB JELLIES

SEA GOOSEBERRY

SALPS

◀▼ Jellyfish swim by gentle jet propulsion. They move slowly through the sea by pumping water from the bell that forms the main part of the body. Even large jellyfishes cannot swim against strong currents and many are cast up on the seashore where they die.

Most jellyfish produce eggs that grow into little polyps. In springtime, their tentacles become smaller and the stem of the body becomes deeply grooved, so that they look like a pile of saucers (see below). In time the "saucers" break away. They are known as ephyra larvae and float off to become the next generation of free-living jellyfish. This method of producing young is called strobilation.

Strange Jellyfish Families

Huge numbers of tiny medusae can sometimes be found floating in the ocean. Each medusa is either male or female and like other animals they produce fertilized eggs. The larvae that hatch from these eggs are not like their parents. They sink to the ocean floor and grow into small polyps. They often look almost like moss growing over a stone. The polyps are neither male nor female and produce young as small growths, or buds, on their bodies. Some of the new "buds" stay attached to their parents. Others float off as new male or female medusae.

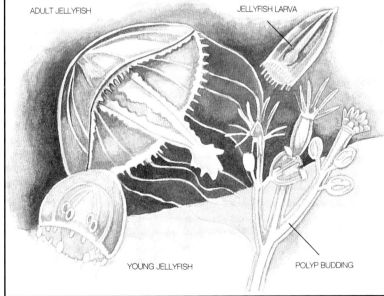

ADULT JELLYFISH

JELLYFISH LARVA

YOUNG JELLYFISH

POLYP BUDDING

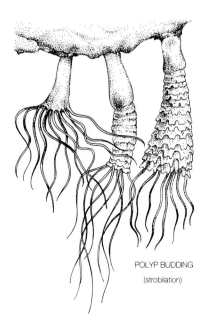

POLYP BUDDING

(strobilation)

EPHYRA LARVAE

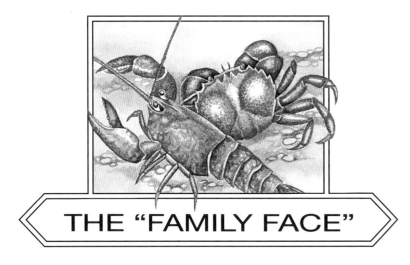

THE "FAMILY FACE"

Young babies often look like their grandparents or more distant relatives. As the child grows, this likeness fades. In a similar way, we can often see a relationship between two apparently different kinds of animals if we look at their larvae.

The larvae we find in the sea often show unexpected relationships between creatures that are otherwise very different. One of the most surprising is the first larva of barnacles. This is called a nauplius. It is very similar to the larvae of crabs and lobsters.

Barnacles, crabs, and lobsters all come from a group of creatures known as crustaceans. It would be difficult to guess that they were related if we were not able to compare their larvae. Other creatures that have similar larvae but very different adults are some of the worms, sea snails, and bivalves. All start life with a larva called a trochophore. After the first stage they develop in different ways to become creatures that look quite unlike each other.

▼ The tiny cowrie shells that live around the coasts of western Europe all look very similar. In fact, there are two different species. The larvae of these two species are quite unlike each other. One has huge, long "water skis" to support it, while the other's are short and rounded. It may be difficult to tell the adults apart, but the larvae are easy to identify.

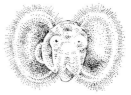

COWRIE LARVAE

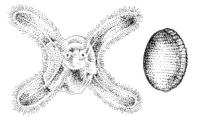

▼ Barnacles are pictured below. Acorn barnacles are covered with hard, sticky plates and live fixed to rocks or other hard objects on the seashore. Goose barnacles have much more fragile armor. They attach themselves to floating objects in the ocean and are part of the plankton, even as adults. Both start their lives as nauplius larvae floating freely in the ocean.

NAUPLIUS BARNACLE LARVA

GOOSE BARNACLES

ACORN BARNACLES

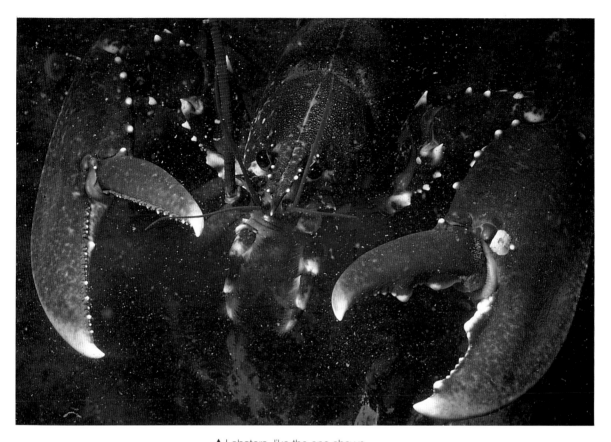

▲ Lobsters, like the one shown above, and all other crustaceans, start life as nauplius larvae. Then they change to become strange-looking creatures, often supported in the water by long spines. They go through several changes before they finally metamorphose into their adult shape. The rest of their lives are spent as heavily armored creatures, living on the ocean bottom.

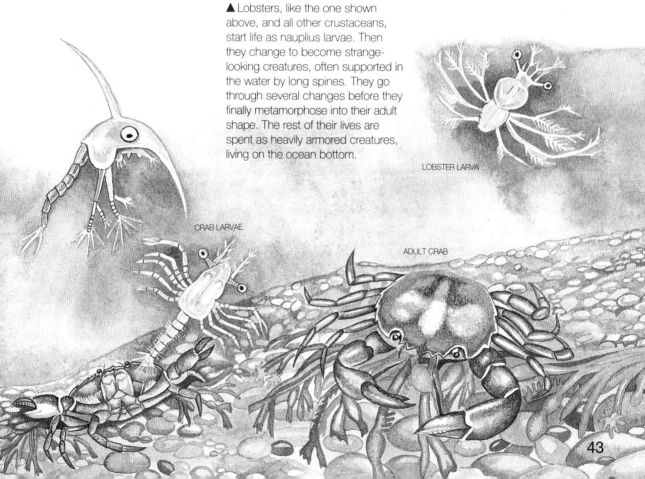

LOBSTER LARVA

CRAB LARVAE

ADULT CRAB

BEYOND LARVAE

Human beings, all other mammals, birds, and reptiles never have larvae. Their young, when born or hatched, look like tiny versions of their parents.

The reason why we and these other animals do not have a larval stage to our lives is that we are protected as we grow. The young of most mammals grow inside the body of the mother. With all birds and most reptiles, the embryo develops within the shelter of a shelled egg. The young of reptiles, birds, and mammals have a better chance of survival because of this protection. The larvae of creatures such as butterflies or sea urchins are not so lucky. Most larvae are eaten by other creatures or killed by natural forces such as bad weather.

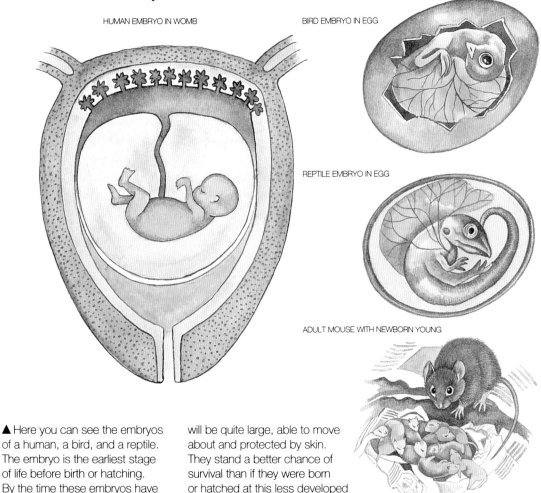

HUMAN EMBRYO IN WOMB

BIRD EMBRYO IN EGG

REPTILE EMBRYO IN EGG

ADULT MOUSE WITH NEWBORN YOUNG

▲ Here you can see the embryos of a human, a bird, and a reptile. The embryo is the earliest stage of life before birth or hatching. By the time these embryos have grown into babies or young, they will be quite large, able to move about and protected by skin. They stand a better chance of survival than if they were born or hatched at this less developed stage.

GLOSSARY

AMPHIBIAN A vertebrate animal. Generally the adults are land-living and breathe air, using small lungs and also their soft, moist skin. The young are water-living tadpoles, which breathe through gills.

CAMOUFLAGE The color or shape of an object or animal that matches the background.

CELLS The microscopically tiny units of which plants and animals are made. Each cell has a membrane around it. Inside is a "command center" called the nucleus. This controls everything that living things do, for example, digestion and growth.

CHRYSALIS The stage in the life of some insects, especially butterflies and moths, in which the changes from larva to adult take place.

CILIA (singular: CILIUM) Fine threads of living matter on the bodies of some animals. Cilia usually beat like tiny oars. They may stabilize or move very small creatures, or make water currents that bring food particles to larger ones.

COCOON The protective covering to some pupae or eggs. Moth pupae and spider eggs usually have cocoons made of silk.

FERTILIZE To fuse male and female cells at mating, so that a new individual may be formed.

GILLS The parts of fishes and other water-living animals that extract oxygen from the environment. They can be compared to the lungs of land animals.

GLANDS Small parts of an animal's body that release chemical messengers into the bloodstream. The effect of these is to alter the animal's behavior in some way.

GRUB A larva.

HABITAT The natural home of a plant or animal. The word often implies a wide area, for example, a forest or a seashore.

HORMONE A chemical produced in small amounts in one part of an animal's body, usually in a gland. It is transported to another part of the body, where it causes a change in the activity of the cells.

HOST An animal or plant that supports and feeds a parasite.

INVERTEBRATE An animal without a skeleton. Some, like worms, are quite soft-bodied. Others, like insects or snails, are supported and protected by a hard outer skeleton or shell.

LARVA (plural: LARVAE) The young of some animals. Larvae are able to fend for themselves, but they usually look different and live and feed differently from their parents. When fully grown, they change fairly rapidly to the adult form.

LIFE CYCLE The series of stages in which an organism passes as it grows.

METAMORPHOSIS The period of rapid change between the larval and adult state. Some insects are referred to as having incomplete metamorphosis because their young stages are not very different in appearance from the adult. Complete metamorphosis involves much greater change, for example, between a caterpillar and a butterfly.

MIGRATE (MIGRATION) The movement of a population of animals from one area to another. Usually there is a return movement later in the year.

MOLT In mammals and birds to molt means to shed hairs and feathers. In many invertebrate animals, molting involves shedding the hard, outer covering of the creature, so that it can increase in size.

NECTAR A sugary substance produced by flowers which attracts pollinators.

NYMPH The young stage of an insect with incomplete metamorphosis.

PARASITE A plant or animal that lives in or on another (its host). The parasite takes food and support, but gives nothing in return.

PARALYZE To affect the nervous system of an animal in some way so that it cannot move.

PLANKTON Animals and plants that float in the currents in lakes or the oceans. Most are small, many are the young stages of bigger creatures.

POLLEN Microscopically small grains that are the male part of seed plants. They are carried by wind, water, or various animals to the female part of a plant of the same species. Fertilization can then take place.

POLLINATE To transfer pollen from one flower to another.

PREDATOR A hunter.

PREY The animals caught and killed by predators.

PUPA (plural: PUPAE) The non-feeding stage in the life of an insect with complete metamorphosis. During this time the animal changes from its larval to its adult form.

RECYCLE To reuse resources.

SPAWN The eggs of amphibians, or fishes, or the act of producing them.

YOLK SAC A sac containing a rich food called yolk that hangs from the under surface of some vertebrate embryos, including many fishes, reptiles, and birds.

INDEX

Illustrations are indicated in **bold**

A TEMPLAR BOOK

Devised and produced by The Templar Company plc
Pippbrook Mill, London Road, Dorking, Surrey RH4 1JE
Copyright © 1991 by The Templar Company plc

PHOTOGRAPHIC CREDITS